My Dear, Dear Stagger Grass

SUSAN LAUGHTER MEYERS

MY DEAR, DEAR STAGGER GRASS

poems

Cider Press Review

San Diego

MY DEAR, DEAR STAGGER GRASS

Cider Press Review
PO BOX 33384
San Diego, CA, USA
CIDERPRESSREVIEW.COM

First edition
10 9 8 7 6 5 4 3 2 1 0

ISBN: 978-1-930781-35-1
Library of Congress Control Number: 2013943553

Cover art, *Georgia Swamp*, bromoil by Gene Laughter
Author photograph by Curtis Rogers
Cover design by Caron Andregg

ABOUT THE CIDER PRESS REVIEW EDITORS PRIZE:

The annual Cider Press Review Editors Prize offers a $1,000 prize, publication, and 25 author's copies of a book-length collection of poetry. For complete guidelines and information, visit CIDERPRESSREVIEW.COM/BOOKAWARD.

Printed in the United States of America
at Thomson-Shore, in Dexter, MI.

for Blue, always —& my brother Gene

Contents

Acknowledgments   vi

I.

Why Does Rain Cast This Longsome Spell?   3
Landmark Inn   4
The Tilt That Stumbles Me   5
Dear Heavy Heart   6
Dear Obligation   7
Merlin's Daughter, Highway 17   8
Season of Tourists   9
Shelling, Hunting Island   11
Coastland   12
Prunus serotina, or Why George   13
Two Friends Hiking at Old Santee Canal   14
Multiple Choice   16
Whistling through My Hands   17

II.

Passage   21
Dear Yellow Speed Bump   22
Morning after the Hailstorm   23
Dear Melancholy   24
Dear Summer of Few Bees   25
Outside Clinton's Barber & Styling Shop   26
April, after Planting   28
Military Maneuvers, South of Drowning Creek   29

Highway 61, after Dark   *30*
My Brother, Last Radiation Treatments   *31*
footnotes, an annotation   *33*
Though I Hold Nothing against Snakes but Fear   *34*
Spell for Setting the Sun   *36*

III.

Letters Lost to Wind   *39*

IV.

Dear Atamasco Lily   *55*
Prothonotary Warblers   *56*
Dear Snakeskin   *57*
Banding Hummingbirds   *58*
After the Funeral   *60*
Why I Am Not a Tightrope Walker   *62*
Light, Its Absence   *63*
Red Hills   *64*
back from the woods inside me   *67*
Oconee Station Falls   *68*
Dear Missing Piece   *70*
One of Those Times   *71*

Notes   *73*

Acknowledgments

Much appreciation goes to the editors of these journals for first publishing the following poems, sometimes in a different version:

Beloit Poetry Journal: Dear Missing Piece
Cave Wall: Landmark Inn; Outside Clinton's Barber & Styling Shop
Cider Press Review: Dear Morning after the Moon Kept Me Awake
Connotation Press: Why Does Rain Cast This Longsome Spell?
Crazyhorse: Spell for Setting the Sun
Ekphrasis: Light, Its Absence
Heron Tree: Dear Abstract Expressionism (as "At Odd Angles Speedily")
jubilat: Dear Heavy Heart; Dear Melancholy
Kakalak, Anthology of Carolina Poets: Whistling through My Hands; Morning after
     the Hailstorm
Lady Jane's Miscellany: *Prunus serotina*, or Why George
Linebreak: Dear Atamasco Lily; Dear Happenstance
North Carolina Literary Review: The Tilt That Stumbles Me; My Brother, Last
     Radiation Treatments; Banding Hummingbirds
The Pedestal: Why I Am Not a Tightrope Walker
Poemeleon: Dear Heavy Traffic; Dear Yellow Speed Bump
Prairie Schooner: Oconee Station Falls; Red Hills; Though I Hold Nothing against
Snakes but Fear
Prime Number: Dear Automated Call System; Dear Constant Barking; Dear Village
     of Mushrooms
Saw Palm, Florida Literature and Art: Coastland
South85: Multiple Choice
South Carolina Review: Shelling, Hunting Island
The Southern Review: One of Those Times
Southern Women's Review: Dear Prothonotary Warblers in the Birdhouse
storySouth: Military Maneuvers, South of Drowning Creek; Passage; Season of
     Tourists
Subtropics: Dear Black-Hooded Parakeets at the Intersection
Tar River Poetry: Dear Loose Wing of a Dragonfly; Dear Snakeskin; Two Friends
     Hiking at Old Santee Canal
Town Creek Poetry: After the Funeral; April, after Planting
Waccamaw, A Journal of Contemporary Literature: Dear Obligation
Wild Goose Poetry Review: Highway 61, after Dark
Yemassee: Prothonotary Warblers

"footnotes, an annotation" appeared in the anthology *Eating Her Wedding Dress: A
Collection of Clothing Poems* (Ragged Sky Press, 2009). "Dear Missing Piece" appeared

in *Boomtown: Explosive Writing from Ten Years of the Queens University of Charlotte MFA Program* (Press 53, 2011).

"Spell for Setting the Sun" appeared on *Verse Daily* at versedaily.com.

"Merlin's Daughter, Highway 17" was first published in the chapbook *Lessons in Leaving* (Persephone Press).

Thanks to the editors of *Cave Wall* for nominating "Landmark Inn" for a Pushcart Prize.

"Oconee Station Falls," "Red Hills," and "Though I Hold Nothing against Snakes but Fear" received the Edward Stanley Award from *Prairie Schooner*. "Prothonotary Warblers" won *Yemassee's* Pocataligo Poetry Prize. "Shelling, Hunting Island" won *South Carolina Review's* inaugural Poetry Prize. "Spell for Setting the Sun" was included in a group of poems that placed as finalist for the *Crazyhorse* Lynda Hull Memorial Prize. "My Brother, Last Radiation Treatments" and "Banding Hummingbirds" were finalists for the 2012 James Applewhite Poetry Prize. "Whistling through My Hands" was a finalist for the *Kakalak* poetry contest.

Special thanks to The Virginia Center for the Creative Arts for time spent there as a Verna Ubben Fellow and to The Poetry Society of South Carolina and Don Ubben, sponsors of the fellowship, for making that residency possible. Also, to the South Carolina State Parks System for time spent in their Artist-in-Residence Program.

To *Cider Press Review* editors Caron Andregg and Ruth Foley, thank you for selecting my manuscript and seeing it, step by step, to its final book form.

My gratitude to friends who graciously spent time reading the manuscript and who, in turn, offered insightful responses and suggestions: Linda Annas Ferguson, Barbara Presnell, Carol Peters, Tom Lombardo, Carol Ann Davis, and Phebe Davidson. I am grateful, too, to Richard Garcia and the Long Table Poets, as well as the Queens Poets critique group and other poet friends too numerous to name, who offered feedback for individual poems. To Barbara G. S. Hagerty, for her eagle eye. And to the many students in classes and workshops who have provided inspiration along the way. Finally, to Blue—for patience and everything good in my life.

The mind derives
from the manifold

concretions and
motions of nature

motions of its own

*

stranger,
hoist your burdens, get on down the road.

—A. R. Ammons

I.

Why Does Rain Cast This Longsome Spell?

My hummingbird's perch, that highest twig,
has no leaves. Today, no bird.
I call the vacancy sorrow.
                        A door ajar:
should I question the necessity of doors?

Last night, one dream warned me
of the other before I woke to a nimbus,
no words to speak of.
                        The mood has fallen,
is still falling. I don't think low pressure
is an accurate term for this weather.

Once, my sister-in-law stood by the sink
while the ice cream melted
                        in its cardboard tub.
Now she insists she has no sister-in-law.

The first dream, like a fissure, had no door.
The second, no windows.

Landmark Inn

Mornings I lounge on the balcony
in my new jeans and good underwear,
below me the river,
                    slow and widening,
green with islands of grass and willows.
Ducks and jays and cowbirds.
                              It's July,
when cicadas own the vacation air.
Here in Tennessee I'm almost happy.
Only the pale domestic goose protests,

but what does she know
about the other side of the mountain,
how it's possible
                  to leave home
and turn away from everything
you call your life, to sit and watch
what wanders into view?

Two mowing machines on the far bank
are slicing the tall grasses birds love
to pick through.
                 Someone from another
balcony throws stale bread, turning
the lawn into a banquet.
A new flock of geese bails out of the sky
with honking, as if to say,
                            Look at me.

And, for these few minutes—
far, far from anyone I know
                            who is dying—I do.

The Tilt That Stumbles Me

I'm driving down the road, by my side a sack
of camellia blossoms and a bee.
The blossoms, their petals silky coins
of pink and red, are stacked and staggered,
some fluted at the edges, some specked with gold.
Beauty heaped in disarray,
though the wrinkled sack lacks all signs of it.
I'm driving down the road with a sack of beauty,
which, I can tell by the buzzing and tapping,
is an ill fit for the bee.
When I pick camellias, I know to hold the blossoms
upside down to free the bees
that may have tunneled deep.
Sometimes the bee does not emerge.
You must learn to look at the world upside down,
the preacher said at Phil's funeral—
the preacher said this clearly, despite his stutter—
the world that will never be the same,
the tilt that stumbles me.
At the light I roll the window down
and open the sack, shaking it and imagining
a kiss of bitterness, and then another, stinging
and singing in circles at my head.
My forehead and nape, the softest
spot on my wrist—they crawl with the song.
But the bee does not emerge.
When the light turns green,
I bear right at Cosgrove—marsh, palmettos,
this sack of beauty. I hear the tapping again,
and again, each time fainter, until no more.

Dear Heavy Heart

Though you are weighted
with lead, sunk this night

to the cold lake bottom
among seasons of skipped stones,

worn and fisted with the old
perplexity of grief,

tomorrow's net, having poked
and fished around

for nothing but oddities
will lift you through air, dripping,

to be eyed and chucked—cheerful—
back to the hot, brambled bank.

Dear Obligation

Your lessons are hard
to unlearn,
my mother in her grave,
my father too,

and still their voices.
*Beauty is as
duty does*, my mother says.
She whispers this

in my ear in the middle of the night,
the same ear, one of them,
she told me to wash behind daily.
There is a train, I hear it rumbling,

and it's always on time.
The word *good* comes up,
often, coupled with instructions
followed by my name.

Merlin's Daughter, Highway 17

The wind beats a silk of blonde
in her eyes, the girl in the truck bed.
She takes her long hair,
twists, twists it to one side.
While her left hand holds it in place,
the right pulls a white hair band
from her pocket.
She stretches it across her fingers—
        she is good at this—
manipulates it one handed
over the twisted hair, pushes it to her neck.
The truck picks up speed.

Now she divides the fluttering handful
into thirds, braids it. Fast.
Over, over, around, over.
        She has done this before—
without a mirror, maybe at school
sitting at her desk in world geography.
She works one handed again,
pulls out another band,
fastens it this time
near the bottom of the braid.
        She is almost done.
Starting at the top, her fingers pat
their way down. They have tamed
every hair but wisps wild at her ears.
She drops both arms, turns
her face to the wind.
Five miles from town,
        and all this, free.

Season of Tourists

Charleston, SC

Say it's October,
after the summer of the bullfrog.
The leaves will soon freefall into the season
of loss, when you will lie there, night after night,
remembering the steady drumming
even though the sound is gone.

In the pond was a statue of bronze—
or was it stone?—now gone.
Not so, the wind sweeping across stone.
Summer, though short,
                    read like a slow refrain,
off-key like the stutter of a slow refrain.
The bullfrog, though only one—
                            and only until July—
thrummed the depths with a low song
you couldn't hum. You keep looking,
listening for the missing. Or was summer
just a rehearsal for shadows?

Wing beats and apologies.
You thought at least one dream
would teach you to fly.
                    The need, that strong.
Like the desire for home. Like the desire
for elsewhere. Unlike the irritable conviction
of the woman ahead of you in line today:

I don't want pretty stamps, she said.
I don't want pretty stamps.
The Post Office shouldn't be in the business

of selling pretty stamps.
            Was her intent to send out
into the world some part of herself unadorned,
to peel away her own affection?

            In a better mood
are the two men and the woman battling
wind at the Battery. No doubt they're glad
for the miles between them and home,
where there's more wind pending.
It's their season.
            What they've missed,
a whole summer, bullfrog to stone,
you can't tell them. There's no sign of it,
and no sign they'd want to know.
            You can hear their glee
in the laughing gulls they're reaching to feed,
see it on their faces,
their tilted heads and fly-away hair.

Shelling, Hunting Island

Some days you find none worth keeping,
not even small cockles,
but you keep looking. Today you pass a woman
sitting on the largest log at the high tide line,
her short brown hair barely lifted by wind,
her shoulders straight, hands limp in her lap.
She ignores the gulls petitioning her ear
and you, invisible as air.
Something is missing, you can tell
by the tilt of her head, her stillness.
Her thighs have each fallen away from the other,
as if emptiness is all
she can make of the morning, as if what she faces
and what she turns her back to
are the same, as if her body is washed up,
but her heart is here to chart the whys
and maybes, here to weigh something
insistent as rain. She doesn't move.
She is the reason you came,
your moon snail, your keyhole limpet,
the lettered olive, and the baby's ear
you won't find. You walk back by, invisible again,
you who have spotted nothing but broken shells,
pearled black and amber,
and this beached stranger, almost your twin,
this woman staring down the sea.

Coastland

When the wind gets up and the water rises,
those who live on higher ground, at a distance
from the pinched smell of pluff mud,
from spartina marshes and swamps of cypress knees,
upland from the tannin-black tributaries
where through the bottoms, among the wet-footed
spider lilies, one barred owl
calls another, one to the other till there's little left to say,
upland from the cottonmouth and the brown water snake
coiled and rooted by the tupelo
and the alligators logging across the slough,
upland from the deer hound pens full of yelps—
full of naps and pacing, full of cedar-thicket dreaming—
and the dirt yard's milling of gray cats
and striped kittens yawning by the palmettos,
upland from the sea sky sea—the horizon
a fine line polished away—
from the shrimp boats shrinking smaller and smaller
on their way to their serious work of gathering,
from the smooth, quick balancing act
of the sun—heavy and orange—riding the waves,
upland from salt myrtle and the season's second growth
of trumpet honeysuckle, those who live at a distance
from the band of quick, dark clouds blooming at sea,
upland from the bang and whirl, clatter
and shake of the wind when it's up,
those who live on higher ground ask
of those who live by the flats and shoals,
the shallows and bogs, *Why,* and again, *Why, O why.*

Prunus serotina, or Why George

He cut it down because on the first
cold night   it wept its sap

            from the trunk's galls,
a thick pool lying
in the lap   of its roots.

He cut it down
        because he had never cut.
Because he was young
and rash   and short
        on consequences.

Because tent caterpillars
            and fall webworms
called its branches   (soon leafless
        and shrouded)   home.

And the thick pool looked like
molasses,   which he refused to taste,

        though politely, a stubbornness
his father protested,
like any good father, but secretly
                    admired.

He cut it down because a hard,
hard lesson   was on the other side
        of cutting—
                    before,
and after,   the lie he wouldn't tell.

Two Friends Hiking at Old Santee Canal

Ahead of me, he balances his feet, left then right,
on the first of two planks—an unsteady bridge of sorts—
laid down for hikers to cross
                         what, on most days,
would be bog,
                but on this one, after weeks of rain, is flooded.

We are learning the look and feel of swamp.

Waiting my turn, I can see his every step.
He pauses halfway across, standing sweaty
in the midst of the ordinary.
                    An inch or so beneath his heels,
under the seam of the two boards,
I see the loops and curves
                of a thick brown snake.
The chiseled head, the slender neck. Above them,
his bare ankles.
            How few, the words we need.
Snake, I say, unable to utter where
                         or put sense to it.
Which way should I go? He is a statue,
his arms frozen in air.
I tell him to come back, and he does.
                    We watch the snake uncurl
and disappear, but in the thrill of fear just past,
our bodies, all breath and jitters, now belong
                to someone we don't recognize.
Forward is the direction we want to choose
but neither of us can step onto the board.
                    We know what we must do:

stumble through ferns and mud,
                              clotted roots, the thick
of mosquitoes, a limestone bluff—
backtrack in the safety of a path already taken.

Multiple Choice

Your chickadee has nested in the wrong house,
exposed and unprotected.

a. You write to it, praising the green
     irony of an open door,
     the breeze that airs the bed.
     Which light, which shadow? you ask.

b. You listen to what could be song
     but sounds more like the scoldings
     of your tap-dancing mind.

c. You breathe in the feathered smell
     of defeat, wondering why you didn't hammer
     the yes-yes-yes closed.

d. At dusk you speak the low syllables of elegy,
     when you can no longer sing.
     You have lost all sight of the tree,
     of whatever trembled its branches.

Whistling through My Hands

Until today, the dove's cry hasn't come
from so deep inside itself since that summer
Emily stepped from the curb into the night's traffic.
She, the troubled bright wonder in our class.

This moment, straight through me because out here
it's closer, my ear a vessel of sorrow?
I want to carry that sound into fall. No, winter.
The morning of her obituary

I went to Paul, our teacher.
Found him in his office and sat there numb
while he cried, that big man at his desk,
his plastic black cat clock behind him on the wall.

Now Paul gone too. I have to remind myself.
If I hollow my hands, clasped together
into the shape of the church
without the steeple, or the people,

line up my thumbs just so,
I can blow on them to make that long, low call
practiced and practiced as a child, till finally
when it came to me, it came to me by heart.

II.

Passage

Forgotten, the first tunnel
I slipped through
      near midnight of that flowering,
the underside of leaves
            a map of mildew.

What did I know of the rose
except a bright bud unfolding?
      Pricked my thumb on a thorn.

Every tunnel I've passed through,
every rose I've cupped in my hand
      to inhale the hour's sweetness,
has brought me here
            to this dwelling place.

Let me say it right.
The first tunnel I slipped through
      was a climbing rose,
            or was it the fire?

I remember now, a smokeless
flame, barely incandescent,
that one small lick of desire.

Dear Yellow Speed Bump

One summer night a friend, on a dare,
played your game with other friends,
lying down across the narrow mountain road
and telling their best secrets. First kiss,

first time at sex. The game went smoothly,
I'm told, and so did the wine, but the secrets
were slow in coming, until one coaxed
the next, fact losing speed to fiction.

If only each day had its defining moment:
a subtle rise to catch a body off-guard
and lift it in serenity or jar it to attention
as we all wheel down the crowded road

trying to get somewhere, anywhere, fast,
when what we really want to do
is lay our burdens down on the loneliest
path and tell our only story to the stars.

Morning after the Hailstorm

On the porch floor the scattered green stars
        that fell   from the sweet gums.
Some torn & misshapen
                    as if to say   the wish
will never come true.   Pine scent
        in the air,
                the gravel drive littered
with pitched needles & limbs.

In the garden the beans
                beaten down,
the herbs (peppers too)   and, oh, the tattered
        umbrellas of squash leaves.

            It was a wild night of lashing,
a veil of steam   rising. All the pummeling
                    & shredding.
All the loose bright green
                    flung
        to the ground,   soon to turn brown.
For a few early hours the tender
                        pretense (forget
the havoc) that the heart is cheerful
        as birdsong. Till the sun,   searing
a different truth,   climbs higher.

Dear Melancholy

Let me start again,
dear gall midge, dear black bile.
At dawn you entered my dream
and I thought the bridge I was crossing
would break in two,
thought the water below
would drink me before I woke
and heard the mourning dove
but only faintly.
I lay there, alone,
until I felt you beside me.
If you were my lover, I'd say
you're faithful. You are not my lover.
I must tend the bait bucket.
The crickets, having sucked
the potato dry, are climbing
the screen wall. A few are dying.
Small news, I know,
and not the sort you wanted to hear.

Dear Summer of Few Bees

You've faded like an old rag draped
too long on the fencepost.

Early, the beans flowered and flowered,
so did the squash.

I wanted to run down the middles,
arms flung, fingers spread, touching

each bloom, anthers to stigma,
but I had no pollen baskets.

You might say I longed for busyness.
The garden stood waiting

in a psalm of diminishment. I tell you
it was a lonely time.

Can't we rent some bees? I asked my husband,
who lacks in patience what I lack

in know-how. You were a long time staying
and didn't harvest a good crop.

Yet, I admit the waiting was worth
something, even waiting for something

that didn't come, even waiting for the small
restlessness meant to deliver good news.

Outside Clinton's Barber & Styling Shop

Georgetown, SC

I'm fond of waiting, anticipation
being better than a party, so I sit in the car,
near the barber pole and window box
of purple pansies, waiting for Blue.

February, the street trees still threaded
with Christmas lights. A couple strolls by,
stopping at store windows as if to memorize
quaintness. At Sal's Shoe Repair

they smile at an old sewing machine
past stitching-in-the-ditch. The building
next to Clinton's needs painting
so the long swipes of rust won't weep

down the wall. The barber shop blinds
are closed. A large woman pauses at the door
to adjust the straw mat with her toe, pointed
like a ballerina's. She goes in,

then a white-haired man. How many
does this little two-window shop hold?
Maybe a crowd's in there clapping, swaying
to the woman's song, dancing on tufts of hair.

I hope Blue doesn't fall and bruise his weak
elbow. Here comes his new crew cut, airy
as a sieve. I like to think he's foreign,
from a country where everything about his day,

even his name, is untranslatable.
I hand him a plastic comb he sticks in his shirt
pocket, mourning the departed hair.
Though his scalp, pink and fastidious,

doesn't show, I can tell he thinks I see through him.
What? he asks, looking puzzled. He never knows
what I'm thinking. I should take advantage
of this moment. I should tell him less than I do.

April, after Planting

You, or the mystery of you, pulled a cart
down the crow path. The cart, full of empties
and premonitions, wobbled its rocky song,
the empties clinking their own clear notes.
I couldn't fault you anymore, despite
the oil stains on your shirt, the one frayed
seam that sliced your pocket to a wider grin.
I stitched the shape of you to the cloudless sky.

Now when I close my eyes, the why of you
rides seamless above the salvia. Hummingbirds
buzz the feeders. At night I pace the garden
and quiz the moon. How to reconcile the stars.
You and your small boat somewhere
daring the wind, me here wishing for rain.

Military Maneuvers, South of Drowning Creek

The sky is pocked with parachutes
raining from the belly
          of the plane,
the fat plane that dropped low
before your windshield
               and now hovers
over the field like a cloud, like a ponderous
thought you could not have predicted.

Or is the sky lit
          by a hundred little suns,
each one sinking to its own twilight?
This unremarkable air,
            a threshold
you can't imagine crossing.

Stop and pay attention, dreamer,
to the weather
          and all that moves.
To timing and the necessity
of risk, to repetition
          and the unrepeatable.
The sky of amber silk is falling.

Highway 61, after Dark

Topography is the best guide.
Memorize each dip and curve,
each ribbon of repair
across this narrow wish leading home.

What you can't see with the low beams
could kill you,
if you don't kill it first.
Live oak, mailbox, live oak, deer—

each sketched in night's charcoal.
Curtains of moss, dingy and torn,
frame a smeared windshield.
Tomorrow, new wiper blades.

Passing headlights, another reason
to tighten your grip, to look beyond
what's nearing, one more glare
you've learned to turn from.

My Brother, Last Radiation Treatments

Summer solstice

All the little runners in my brain,
wearing their best sneakers, have readied themselves.
It's time: *On your mark.* The days grow shorter,
another way to measure.

A wasp investigating the window frame
takes light for granted. In the lowest limb of a pine
a red-tailed hawk moves nothing but head
and eye, every blink an aperture closing.

Yesterday my brother sent photos
he took years ago—one of me, the youngest,
drinking from the fountain at Fontana Dam.
I squint and reach, barely tall enough.
How well I remember the dress, the soft ribbon
of water cooling my lips.

                All the little runners
want a story about the boy, his first camera—
boy of few words—how he, fifteen
and snapping close-ups, learned the art.
How that summer he took to the woods
where he made a white bracelet of snake rattles.
Other summers he took to the beach. Lifeguarding.
That tan and peroxided boy, that tall shutterbug.

The coneflowers out back, their petals
at odd angles, look picture pretty and casual enough
to be on vacation.
                Mostly sunny and warm.
The little runners, panting—all of them—

are in sight of the last turn. Home stretch,
though a dark blur just shot past them,
a small thing preyed upon, or closing in on prey.

footnotes, an annotation

[1] *Goody two-shoes*, overly cheerful
    person who started out
        with one shoe but now has two.
    And they match, goody goody.

[2] *Pigeon-toed,* first used in 1801.
    Scandalous,
        those red sandals
    (T-strapped and buckled) pinching
    the tender grass
        barely.

[3] The foot has 26 bones, one fewer than the hand.
    So what, if sneakers
        kick their way down the trail,
    tatting up   old leaves?

[4] Achilles, unpopular name for a dog.
    From hearth to snow (see also *ice*)
    fur-lined clogs   click
    their soles, toggle on
        and off.

[5] *Toehold:* a wrestling move.
    Hip boots, tough enough to battle
    surprise—
        say, a wakening
    of snakes.

Though I Hold Nothing against Snakes but Fear

From out the dark door of the secret earth.
                                    —D. H. Lawrence

I say to my husband, *Get a knife.* I say that.
The dying water snake, fat as a rope, a rhythm of bulges,
but from what?   I guess fish, then frogs.
Make up your mind, he says. *Frogs.*   The rest is silence

until his knife, sliding down the bright belly,
makes a ripping sound. This is after   the snake is shot
and pulled from the rock pile rimming the pond—
        he did it for me
                        or if not for me,
        a perception of me—
after it's flung into the wheelbarrow   where it writhes,
but only slightly,   even now, when slit down the belly,
even now   when the gray sacks of baby snakes
are scraped out.
                        The mother snake
writhes once or twice more,   but only slightly,
until the sting of gasoline.

That's when she pulses into a braid,   tighter and tighter,
tail thrashing,   hard, against metal, her mouth
working open and closed.
                        I know better,
                                and so does he
despite old farm ways of drenching hornets and bees.
What is it we think we need   to be rid of?
                        We both know better.

With my fingernail I dig into the cuticle of my thumb

until it bleeds.   The sun, still shining,
and the belly now rinsed of red.

Dark between the rocks.   Unsettled, too,
the fish in the pond,   lipping the water's surface.
        Who owns this place anyway?
                        Ours,   not ours.
The snake lies dead in the wheelbarrow,
and all the little snakes.   Fifteen, I counted.
Something flies are attracted to,   no longer fit
                        for vultures or crows.

Once I could say I had never harmed a snake.
Along a wooded trail I'm one who prays
                        for a divide
between my path   and where a snake intends to be.
I who admired the bright orange,
        the orange leather of the belly
                        and the striped jelly
of the babies that,   before the gasoline,
had just begun to wriggle.

            I go inside in an unforgiving mood
and look out the sunroom window,   surprised
the pond is still there,
                        its rocks, water lilies in bloom,
a few white disks of hibiscus.

Spell for Setting the Sun

Be slantwise on bark. Hammered
by shadows longer than want.
So what if the day turns to dry toast

and fetterbush? I'm sorry
for envy, sorry for lies.
Be slantwise on bark. Be bitten

in half. Peachglow then waferless,
the tide going out. A rinse
of apricot gone from the sky.

I'm sorry for thievery, sorry for pride.
Be bitten in half. Be juiceless
and dead, night's bold erasure. Kin

to the cloud-eaten moon. The dark
between stepping stones, a hole
in my sky. Be juiceless, be dead.

III.

Letters Lost to Wind

*

Dear Happenstance

Last night I dreamed you
lost as an old shoe lying,
strings untied, on the macadam.

I'm speeding down the road,
and you are everywhere I look:
brushy bluestem, thick with abandon.

Dented mailbox, gravel drive,
fake flowers nailed
to the tree trunk at the curve.

A flock of small birds
darkens with synchronized turning.
Silvers, veering back again.

[Dear Birdless Trees ...]   [Dear Something Ventured ...]   [Dear Billboard ...]

Dear Heavy Traffic

Mornings I rise and hear you faintly,
close my eyes to pretend you're the sea.
Wave after wave, swells and lulls.

Once in the marsh spoonbills flew over me,
their wings a dream of improbable pinks.
Hard to quit looking. The only sound a whistle

of willets. I stood there meaning to forget
every stalled moment of you—headlight,
taillight, a chain of stops and starts.

But the birds, the arc of their flight,
how could I distance myself from coming
and going? Dear road hum, is it wrong,

this mute longing? I fill the shallows
with spoonbills. A given, their rhythm.
At low tide their heads troll greenly side to side.

[Dear Mistaken Identity ...]   [Dear Whatever It Takes ...]

Dear Prothonotary Warblers in the Birdhouse

Nothing satisfies hunger like dull habit
pinched in the mouth of beauty.

Awed by your recent shelling?
Lost like a new moon?

What matters to you comes and goes, full
of what matters more, then empty.

Long, gaping desire: beware of.

All music in these woods is sweet,
sweet to somebody.

Night, when all isn't.

Soon—I can't tell you, and you can't imagine—
the widening.

This cup of moss, a feathering.
Tomorrow, the swamp's solitary hour.

Believe me, that small sun you're privy to,
there is more light than.

[Dear Thicket of Brambles …]   *[Dear Fledged Hunger …]*

Dear Village of Mushrooms

Each morning this week I've gasped
at the change. You I wake for:
daily your countless possibilities—

high and higher still, till I fear
the worst. What sludge
speculation can yield,
              what winged worries.
The rain lilies near the path bend low.
A snakeskin twists
through the grill of the fire pit,

pale reminder of what? I know
where screech owls once whinnied
at dusk—not far from you—

and which trees, a little to the south,
the webworm favors. Who's to say
when the season will peak and when

first frost. The goldenrod glows
and the salt myrtle is turning
to a sea of white.
              Through your shade,
my dear pagodas, all day I've threaded
forgetfulness. Is that enough?
I will look for you again tomorrow.

[Dear Small Caution …]   [Dear Thimbleweed …]   [Dear I Told You So …]

Dear Indefatigable Blue

Carnivals envy your wide lap,
its needful valley.
                    Or does the cardinal
swoon over your appetite
and wingspan?

You shake out cleanly like a tablecloth.

Hucksters turn wary, gymnasts
topple, dogs slobber and pant.

Yellow jackets have lost their will
to sting.
        Whatever peppers morning,
ground to essentials, will stay
to make a habit of yearning.

Whatever spills
on your good side, seeping
                    between weavings,
will remain of you a fruitful part.

[Dear Faded Sonata …]   [Dear Bittermint …]

Dear Abstract Expressionism

the smallest bird threading the tea olive
I'm calling   blue-gray gnat-

catcher on a hunch   as the little birds weave
in & out   too wary & nimble for naming

with the same quick circuity   thoughts
flit through   though they sometimes collide

not necessarily heeding light   or proximity
you know the rules   or the hint of them

something like the long suspension
of carpenter bees   holding & drifting

up down & sideways   dipping
& rising at odd angles speedily

to that perfect circle   meanwhile the crow's
shadow has passed over   hugely   twice

[Dear Supplejack …]   [Dear False Nettle …]

Dear Hamlet

you waltz like carpenter
bees under rafters

two bees
or not two bees but five

so moodily have crooked
a path soon a hole

otherwise an excavation
too loudly to be missed

reason! reason!
wink off this ocean

of tears casting a quarrelsome other
but sad north-northeast

have you lies?
could you grieve? to bleed

and fatten on this floor
to have loved most loyally

a beeline
mollifies the dark and ire of it

[Dear Obedience …]   [Dear Try, Try Again …]   [Dear Upstart Crow …]

Dear Spelling Bee

You are a cross pollination of jitters
& satisfaction, before & after the hush:

for the sake of syllabicity,
for the sake of etymology, for the sake

of the smithery whole.
Such joinery whips up a swarm.

Your orthographic path is abuzz
with rules to keep & the brief

awful stops, one stop concatenated
to the next. Barely time for a sip

of air. Suspense is no balm.
Hear the drone of prayers to memory?

The dizziest have fallen like beelzebubs,
a plethora of fidget, blunder & sting.

Only one is winged & bejeweled—privy
to singulars & plurals, prefixes

& suffixes sweet enough to fructify.

[Dear Weather Forecast ...]   *[Dear Nevertheless ...]*

Dear Loose Wing of a Dragonfly

Anyone ever call you autumn's mother
of pearl, stained
                glass pane,   translucence
threaded with your own inked lines?
One of you without the other
obligates the mind.   Debris: scant
though never meager, a sliver,
                twin to the willow oak's
fallen leaf. Left drifting
          in the wind   unhinged,
parchment waiting for
weather to write a final testament.
Devil's needle
        with nothing left to darn.

[Dear Resurrection Fern …]   *[Dear Dog-Hobble …]*

Dear Constant Barking

Afraid none can parse
your one request?

Consider the clouds, cumulus
and lacking the urgency of crows.

You could practice crowlessness.
Better yet, study harmonics.

Even wind chimes, plinking,
syncopate their notes.

Your persistence, a sign of—what?
Fire and ice. Nagging:

the phone ringing, the tea kettle's
whistle, a child's tug at the sleeve.

I'm beginning to feel bad
for stutter dog. No, starting to think

you could practice forgiveness
until there's no one left to forgive.

Then what good your refrain?
Old lessons ride the air:

less is, put your money where,
do unto, catch more flies with.

[Dear Loneliness …]   [Dear Feverfew …]

Dear Automated Call System

Let me guess: you've been going to therapy
for passive-aggressive behavior.

I'll guess again: holding back
my chance, making me wait,

you're in a state of denial
and I'm the dog you won't feed.

Yesterday I forgot my dead mother's birthday.
There's hope for me yet.

Last night frost turned the red maple
buds brown. Frost, always full of surprise.

Time is on no one's side, and drought
is forecast again for summer.

I used to be a good speller,
does that count?

I used to sketch parakeets,
does that count more?

One of us in the house got a haircut,
the other refuses to use the phone.

[Dear Indeterminacy …]   [Dear Ten Miles over the Speed Limit …]

Dear Morning after the Moon Kept Me Awake

Last night's monocle
split to pieces by the loblolly limbs,

wind at the window secretive
as an owl
      at woods edge,
an ear tuned to the groundlings
on guard in the switchgrass.

Your promise, sweet daydream:
drowsy inexactitude
           a few degrees up
from chill, a rapt vigil,
sleep no longer fretworthy,

a shadow half shadow that shadow—

you, darling daybreak, accountable
for eyeshot greening & winged.

[Dear Twayblade …]   [Dear Rain Refusing to Fall …] [Dear Exit 150 …]

Dear Black-Hooded Parakeets at the Intersection

The dark-&-slightest-green of you
mimics pigeons on the wire.

Against the light I can't tell
and habit's got the best of me

until I look again and see, I swear,
not pigeons but a sudden flutter

of pistachios, limes, tourmaline
bandits caped and quilled—

bright, then brighter, filling the sky.
I'm arrival and departure.

Foolish doubletake, cautionless
and agog. You are morning, its jig

of surprise, hello-goodbye,
hallelujah free and featherborne.

*

IV.

Dear Atamasco Lily

Nothing else in the swamp rises beyond
the surprise of you
                and your sweet repetition.

Your boldness I'd expect of the cottonmouth
sunning by the bald cypress,

your plenitude matched only
                        by last year's
tent caterpillars, whose droppings
when they fell
                ticked a steady shower.

And what of the music in your name,
hiding your poison?

You are danger, deep-throated cup
lipping the stippled light,
                brightening the leaf mold.

        Dear red-stained lily. Rain lily.
Zephyr lily. Dear fairy lily.
                        Wild Easter lily.
My dear, dear stagger grass.

Prothonotary Warblers

Because it was getting dark, he duct-taped
the birdhouse hole, though the snake
was too fat to climb back out anyway.
This morning he kills it with a hoe.

Revenge, he says. This time I don't flinch.
This time I take the knife
and rip the snake open myself,
its mouth already a wide gap of surprise.

Just as we guessed, the snake is full
of baby warblers, four of them, stinking
and all skin except for the stiff, damp
beginnings of feathers at wing's end.

He flings the snake over the gate,
and by the time we return from town
with a metal baffle
we should have bought years ago

vultures have come and gone,
claiming for their own
a snake which had already laid claim
to the promise that, in weeks to come,

the woods would thicken
with new song fledged in yellow.

Dear Snakeskin

Perfect, your memory
of the body

      whose duties
you've shed the weight of:
say, hunting
past the season of plenty.

I came upon you
      with a shiver,

not from danger
but the memory of danger.

      The first day
I came upon you whole.
By the second day
you were a suggestion
of the suggestion of a body

more missing than matter.

You who hold nothing
hold sway over me—

you, now nothing
      but tatter.

Banding Hummingbirds

San Pedro River, Arizona

I, who know little of ornithology,
wear sticker number nineteen. This release,
the last of the day, is mine. Under the awning
the ornithologist at the table puts a straw to her lips
and blows, parting the feathers to check for mites.
There are mites.

She cradles the bird in one hand,
sexes it, names the species (Anna's), and figures
the approximate age. Places it in a miniature sling
and weighs it, wraps the metal band around one leg.
I walk over to the designated grassy area,
both hands in my pockets.

The day is raw.
When it's time, I hold out a palm, now warm.
The assistant fits the tubes of a stethoscope
to my ears, pressing the disc against my bird.
I hear a low whir, a tiny motor running in my hand.
Up to twelve hundred beats a minute, she says.

I, who know so little,
barely take a breath. My bird's head is a knob
of red iridescence on the fleshy pad of my hand.
I am nothing but a convenient warming bench,
yet for now I am that bench. Warm.
His breast is thin—bone hollow, she says,

where he should be round.
His eyes dark and still, his feet tucked
behind his body. He lies there, that tiny motor.
I don't think of years ago, my mother, my father—
those I loved who, having lain down, never rose up.
For once, I know the worth,

at least to me. What I don't know
is whether this bird in hand will rouse
the way he did earlier, pinched between thumb
and index finger and tipped toward a feeder,
when he drank with conspicuous hunger.
You could see the tongue.

After the Funeral

Crossing a swinging bridge
over the gorge—

that's what it feels like,
every tree you see

far away, untouchable,
one indistinguishable from the other.

Where to rest your eyes,
though not for long,

this brevity of wishing
for more ground and less air.

Someplace to land,
pulling something close,

pushing something away.
The tender balance,

what belongs, what used to belong,
what glimmers like water,

what stands out—leaves
losing their color early

or sunlight on painted rails.
The child in front of you

runs without fear, older than you
the first time you were here.

Wind blows in your face,
blows above you and below.

Why I Am Not a Tightrope Walker

Furthermore, I'm afraid of swinging bridges.
Not to mention cliffs
          and whitewater rapids.
The whole vacation equaled two weeks
of balancing in air,
          what daredevils live for.
I am no daredevil.
The Painted Desert, though,
            was another story.
At every turn I said, *This is it. The scenery
can't get any better,*
          and then we rounded
another bend, and it did. The pinks.
No, the rusts.
      No, the shades between, the ones
I can't name. The memory matters
more now, if that's possible,
            than the real thing
did to me then, and it meant a lot then.
I sit at home, in the backyard
            by the sweet bay,
watching the goldfish circle their world,
and once in a while
         I prop my feet,
close my eyes, and go there.
The pinks again. The palest of yellows.

Light, Its Absence

I should have schooled my one good turkey,
taught him how to come in from the rain.
I would have crossed two fields—early corn
and butter beans—and shooed him to the pen
had I known the distraction of grass, a bee,

worms, the seduction of dirt. Not chickens
or guineas, but my lone turkey—red-lidded
pot of ash, feather duster, gobbler of plenty
under a pink bowl of sky, peck-peck-pecking
at the inexhaustible day. A sudden drowning

of color: pink turned gray turned unremarkably
black; when even crows head for cover;
when all the weather calls for is good sense
and speed; when the answer, close by, is tree,
shed, light—whatever can save whatever is lost.

Red Hills

I come to these hills ready to be lost.
Tell me which path: shadow
of quick decisions,
                    shadow of no sleep.
I take shadow to mean the blue weariness
of doubt. I take light for what it is,
absence no one objects to.

Some moments are that clear, a loose weave
draped flawlessly across the day.
How to shoulder the weight,
part memory, part grudge?
                    A day of walking
it'll take to shake this old umbrage.
Some paths are erasures,

bird, tree, stone no longer there
or no longer wished for. Forget the path
and let the slope stand for slope.
A slight curve,
                call it a valley,
like the one behind a bent knee.
Think of the past and feel bathed in it.

The game was hide and seek,
when in the vast neighborhood
all but one
        would hide.
Dusk, when the stakes were high
if you were the one seeking.
A face I once loved wore its blank look,

a gaze that gazed beyond me: the sort
of fixity
      you'd expect from a landscape.
A woman could choose to come here
not to see deeply into her life
but to spread it out like a map.
She could chart its topography

and still know nothing
of what rides above it.
She could turn from town
toward these unpeopled, chatterless hills
and make them her own.
                  Easy to forgive
the slope its rise and fall.

Isn't that the beauty, one thing slightly
above, or below, the rest—
              oblique?
The woman could name these hills
as if they were tameable as children.
Say, Sleeps in the Sun
or Youngest Who Fidgets.
                Once she speaks

the words for each, hard to turn her back.
Hills hunched like slumbering animals,
their stories accumulated and untold.
The oldest begins with sunlight,
in a soft pitch rising,
         rust and red,
uninitiated, open to what the day unfolds.

Let the wind shift the sands, let the hills

be creased and creviced.
I say that as if I were some god
building something
from nothing.
        What I meant to say:
Let these red hills be enough.

back from the woods inside me

back from the woods   inside me
chickadee silence

nothing I can say to myself   so full
the not saying

when I opened the nesting box
what looked slight

plain yet right   filled the moment
spilling over into what once was

and what might be
their warm bodies feathered out

their eyes on me quick
with fright   the luck of finding two

small birds   one turned east
and the other west   as if placed

that way   to remind me where
I'd come from where I was going

Oconee Station Falls

Trailhead sign: Bears have been
sighted frequently in this area.

Because I came alone,
forgot my bear bell
            and all bears like warning,
because the trail is long and, occasionally, steep.

Because the crow's wing
is a flag flapping in heavy wind
and I am tired of singing.

What good this frail walking stick?
What good my song?

If I stoop to admire the orange-throated mushroom
do I turn my back?
Thunder. And drops
            smacking the path.
Which is worse, the too-frequent bear
or the too-close lightning with tattoo of rain?
Two-thirds of the way there
                and good sense says
                turn around.
I am an old woman needing comfort,
needing sunlight and birdsong, the falls.
One glimpse of the falls.

Some things cannot be cast behind.

Hard to walk fast enough, singing
and talking away thunder,

              the too-frequent bear.
In my heart, this thunder.
From nowhere, believe me, this bear.

Dear Missing Piece

Here's the gray shape of you,
where you're supposed to be
while off somewhere else.

Colorful and jigsaw,
but loose—I could say useless—
as a hat on a headless mannequin.

A hen clucks come morning,
the egg gone, the nest
pressed to the curve of egg.

Rare, the prodigal returning, tired
of being apart—
adjoined: O body, O heart.

One of Those Times

It's like standing on a precipice,
wind blowing—need I tell you
from which direction?—hard, urging me
to forget all I've grown used to,
the hours of sky I've wished into turquoise,
the long climb up
                and the sudden slippings too,
the hours I like to sit and do nothing,
stubbornness and a predilection for *no*.
The wind keeps blowing and the dirt under my feet
crumbles away, while I, for once lined up
body to soul without quarrel,
think of the time I was four
pedaling my tricycle down the slate walk
fast as my legs would go, hedge a blur on one side,
red maples on the other, that fast, or so it seemed,
until I reached the little bridge over the ditch,
a narrow arch so new it still smelled of wood.
One of those times I couldn't stop myself
yet couldn't keep going without a fall.
Scattered scars to prove it.
                That's not the point.
I stand on a precipice, wanting to kneel,
to fold up like a clean, white handkerchief
that fits in a pocket, to flick off every speck
of grit, half the wrongs and recriminations.
My hand is poised, the favored one
that taps three fingers when impatient,
the greedy one that reaches for what bears taking.
I bend to brush something away,

but there's the shifting underfoot and the wind,
believable, nagging at my ear,
telling back to me all my old, sweet lies.

Notes

The quotations by A. R. Ammons are from two of his poems: "Sparklings," from *Brink Road*. Copyright © 1996 by A. R. Ammons. "Gravelly Run," from *The Selected Poems of A. R. Ammons: Expanded Edition*. Copyright © 1986 by A. R. Ammons. Both are used by permission of W. W. Norton & Company, Inc.

"Passage" was inspired by T. S. Eliot's *The Dry Salvages*.

"Light, Its Absence" was written after viewing *Girl with Turkeys, Giverny* (1886), by Theodore Wendel.

"Whistling through My Hands" is in memory of my first poetry teacher, Paul Rice.

"My Brother, Last Radiation Treatments" is for Gene.

"Red Hills" was inspired by the painting of the same name by Georgia O'Keeffe.